vegetables

simple and delicious easy-to-make recipes

Bernice Hurst

p

This is a Parragon Publishing Book
First published in 2002

Parragon Publishing
Queen Street House
4 Queen Street
Bath, BA1 1HE, UK

ISBN: 0-75258-900-8

Printed in China

Produced by the Bridgewater Book Company Ltd.

Photographer Ian Parsons

Home Economist Sara Hesketh

NOTES FOR THE READER

- This book uses both imperial and metric measurements. Follow the same units of measurement throughout; do not mix imperial and metric.

- All spoon measurements are level: teaspoons are assumed to be 5 ml, and tablespoons are assumed to be 15 ml.

- Unless otherwise stated, milk is assumed to be whole milk, eggs and individual vegetables such as carrots are medium, and pepper is freshly ground black pepper.

- Recipes using raw eggs should be avoided by infants, the elderly, pregnant women, convalescents, and anyone suffering from an illness.

- The times given are an approximate guide only. Preparation times differ according to the techniques used by different people and the cooking times may also vary from those given. Optional ingredients, variations, or serving suggestions have not been included in the calculations.

contents

introduction

Vegetables provide an opportunity for adventure in the kitchen. Selecting, cooking, and eating them are very satisfying. With just a small yard, patio, or even a sunny window ledge, we can even produce them ourselves—enjoying the pleasure of planting, nurturing, and, finally, presenting our homegrown food at table.

Alternatively, we can go to the market or supermarket and select from a range of bright, colorful, familiar, or exotic specimens, mulling over their colors and shapes while planning how to make best use of their taste, texture, and eye-appeal. Nowadays, we are no longer dependent on seasons and can select from the world's best—and most intriguing—produce at any time of year.

This book presents some simple and delicious ideas for vegetable cookery, from traditional to contemporary. We have kept the instructions simple and avoided stating the obvious, such as telling you to peel an onion or giving instructions for boiling eggs. But where fruit and vegetables have to be peeled or seeded we have said so, unless (as with onions) they are rarely used unpeeled.

guide to recipe key		
	easy	Recipes are graded as follows: 1 pea = easy; 2 peas = very easy; 3 peas = extremely easy.
	serves 4	Recipes generally serve four people. Simply halve the ingredients to serve two, taking care not to mix imperial and metric measurements.
	10 minutes	Preparation time.
	20 minutes	Cooking time. Where additional chilling or resting times are involved, these times have been added on separately: eg, 15 minutes + 30 minutes resting time

nutty beet salad
page 18

bell peppers stuffed with rice & corn
page 40

classic roast vegetables
page 58

brussels sprouts with chestnuts
page 88

soups, appetizers & salads

Soups, appetizers, and salads are all composite dishes that can be served either to whet the appetite or to provide a substantial meal in themselves. They can be hot or cold, made from just two or three ingredients, or a mixture of anything and everything that comes to hand. Even when served as accompaniments, though, they should be treated with respect and presented in the most attractive way possible. Choose from a tasty and appealing range of dishes, from Cauliflower & Olive Salad and Sunflower Carrot Slaw to mouthwatering Chilled Pea Soup and Nutty Beet Salad.

cauliflower
& olive salad

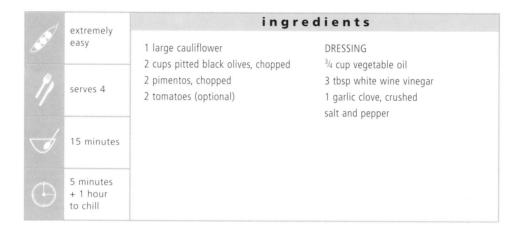

		ingredients	
extremely easy		1 large cauliflower	DRESSING
		2 cups pitted black olives, chopped	¾ cup vegetable oil
serves 4		2 pimentos, chopped	3 tbsp white wine vinegar
		2 tomatoes (optional)	1 garlic clove, crushed
15 minutes			salt and pepper
5 minutes + 1 hour to chill			

Separate the cauliflower florets. Cook in a large pan of salted boiling water for about 5 minutes, or until just tender. Drain well.

Combine the cauliflower, olives, and pimentos in a large bowl. If using tomatoes, cut them into fourths, remove the seeds, chop the flesh, and mix in with the other vegetables.

Place all the dressing ingredients in a jar with a screw-top lid. Shake well. Pour the dressing over the cauliflower and toss gently to coat. Cover with plastic wrap and chill for at least 1 hour.

Remove from the refrigerator 10 minutes before serving. Stir once more, then transfer to a serving dish.

sunflower
carrot slaw

very easy	**ingredients**
serves 4–6	1 lb/450 g carrots pinch of sugar (optional) ¾ cup mayonnaise 1 tbsp lemon juice (optional) 2 tbsp sunflower seeds salt and pepper 4 tbsp chopped fresh parsley chopped fresh parsley, to garnish
5 minutes	
1 hour to chill	

Peel and finely grate the carrots.

Combine the grated carrot, mayonnaise, sunflower seeds, and parsley (together with a pinch of sugar and the lemon juice if you like) in a large mixing bowl. Season to taste.

Cover with plastic wrap and chill for at least 1 hour. When ready to serve, mix thoroughly and transfer to an attractive bowl or carefully spoon on to the side of each individual plate. Garnish with chopped parsley.

chilled pea soup

		ingredients	

easy		scant 2 cups chicken or vegetable
		  stock or water
		4 cups frozen peas
		4 scallions
		salt and pepper
		1¼ cups plain yogurt
		  or light cream
			GARNISH
			2 tbsp chopped fresh mint, scallions
			  or chives
			grated lemon rind

serves 3–4			
5 minutes			
5 minutes + 2–3 hours to chill			

Bring the stock to a boil in a large pan over medium heat. Reduce the heat, add the peas and scallions and simmer for 5 minutes.

Cool slightly, then strain twice, making sure that you remove any pieces of skin. Pour into a large bowl, season to taste, and stir in the yogurt or cream. Cover the bowl with plastic wrap and chill for several hours in the refrigerator.

To serve, remove from the refrigerator, mix well, and ladle into a large tureen or individual soup bowls or mugs. Garnish with chopped mint, scallions or chives, and grated lemon rind.

green bean
& walnut salad

		ingredients	
	very easy	1 lb/450 g green beans	DRESSING
		1 small onion, finely chopped	6 tbsp olive oil
	serves 2 as an appetizer or 4 as a side dish	1 garlic clove, chopped	2 tbsp white wine vinegar
		4 tbsp freshly grated Parmesan cheese	salt and pepper
			2 tsp chopped fresh tarragon
	10 minutes		2 tbsp chopped walnuts or almonds, to garnish
	5 minutes + 30 minutes to chill		

Trim the beans, but leave them whole. Cook for 3–4 minutes in salted boiling water. Drain well, refresh under cold running water, and drain again. Put into a mixing bowl and add the onion, garlic, and cheese.

Place the dressing ingredients in a jar with a screw-top lid. Shake well. Pour the dressing over the salad and toss gently to coat. Cover with plastic wrap and chill for at least 30 minutes.

Remove the beans from the refrigerator 10 minutes before serving. Give them a quick stir and transfer to an attractive, shallow serving dish.

Toast the nuts in a dry skillet over medium heat for 2 minutes, or until they begin to brown. Sprinkle the toasted nuts over the beans to garnish before serving.

red onion,
tomato & herb salad

		ingredients	

extremely easy	2 lb/900 g tomatoes, sliced thinly
	1 tbsp sugar, optional
	salt and pepper
	1 red onion, sliced thinly into rings
	large handful coarsely chopped
	   fresh herbs
		DRESSING
		2–4 tbsp vegetable oil
		2 tbsp red wine vinegar or
		   fruit vinegar	

serves 4 as an appetizer, 6 as a side dish			
10 minutes			
20 minutes to chill			

Arrange the tomato slices in a shallow bowl. Sprinkle with sugar (if using), salt, and pepper.

Separate the onion slices into rings and sprinkle them over the tomatoes. Sprinkle the herbs over the top. Any fresh herbs that are in season can be used—for example, tarragon, sorrel, cilantro, or basil.

Place the dressing ingredients in a jar with a screw-top lid. Shake well. Pour the dressing over the salad and mix gently.

Cover with plastic wrap and chill for 20 minutes. Remove the salad from the refrigerator 5 minutes before serving, unwrap the dish, and stir gently before setting out on the table.

nutty beet salad

		ingredients	
	very easy	3 tbsp red wine vinegar or fruit vinegar	DRESSING ¼ cup plain yogurt
	serves 4	3 cooked beets, grated 2 sharp eating apples 2 tbsp lemon juice	¼ cup mayonnaise 1 garlic clove, chopped 1 tbsp chopped fresh dill salt and pepper
	15 minutes		TO SERVE 4 large handfuls mixed salad greens 4 tbsp pecans
	4 hours to chill		

Sprinkle vinegar over the beets, cover with plastic wrap, and chill for at least 4 hours.

Core and slice the apples, place the slices in a dish, and sprinkle with the lemon juice.

Combine the dressing ingredients in a small bowl. Remove the beets from the refrigerator and dress. Add the apples to the beets and mix gently to coat with the salad dressing.

To serve, arrange a handful of salad greens on each plate and top with a large spoonful of the apple and beet mixture.

Toast the pecans in a heavy, dry skillet over medium heat for 2 minutes, or until they begin to brown. Sprinkle them over the beets and apple to garnish.

main courses

You don't have to be a committed vegetarian to enjoy vegetables as a main course. Taking advantage of fresh seasonal produce can and should prove inspirational. Throw away preconceived notions about lentils, beans, and nut loaves and concentrate instead on color, flavor, and texture. Despite what you may think, there is no limit to the creative possibilities of vegetarian food—and delicious, healthy, filling meals can be produced with the minimum of effort.

summer
spanish omelet

		ingredients	
very easy	½ cup butter		8 extra large eggs
	1 small onion, chopped		4 tbsp milk
serves 4	1 cup cooked potatoes (diced)		1 tbsp tomato paste
	or cooked pasta		salt and pepper
	½ cup cooked peas, corn,		1½ cups grated strong cheese
	or diced zucchini		
10 minutes	4 stalks asparagus, cooked and		bread and salad to serve
	cut into 1 inch/2.5 cm pieces,		
10 minutes	or		
+ 5 minutes	½ cup cooked chopped spinach		
resting time			

Melt the butter over medium heat in a large skillet. Add the onion, stir well, and cook for 3–4 minutes, until soft.

Mix in the potato or pasta and remaining vegetables and cook for a 2 minutes more to heat through.

Beat the eggs with milk, tomato paste, salt, and pepper. Pour the egg mixture over the vegetables and reduce the heat to low. Cook, occasionally lifting the edges and tilting the skillet to let the liquid run.

Preheat the broiler to high. When the eggs are almost set, sprinkle in the cheese. Place the skillet under the broiler and cook for 2 minutes, or until the cheese has melted and is golden brown.

Remove the skillet from the broiler and let the omelet rest for 5 minutes. Transfer to a large serving dish and serve, cut in wedges, with salad and fresh crusty bread.

leek & egg mornay

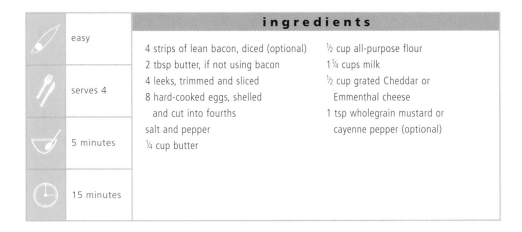

easy	
serves 4	
5 minutes	
15 minutes	

ingredients

4 strips of lean bacon, diced (optional)
2 tbsp butter, if not using bacon
4 leeks, trimmed and sliced
8 hard-cooked eggs, shelled
   and cut into fourths
salt and pepper
¼ cup butter

½ cup all-purpose flour
1¼ cups milk
½ cup grated Cheddar or
   Emmenthal cheese
1 tsp wholegrain mustard or
   cayenne pepper (optional)

Cook the bacon (if using) in a small skillet over medium heat until crisp. Remove from the skillet and sprinkle over the bottom of a large, shallow ovenproof dish, leaving the fat in the skillet.

Cook the leeks in the bacon fat or in 2 tablespoons of melted butter. Remove when soft and combine with the bacon. Arrange the egg wedges on top and season to taste.

Preheat the broiler to high.

Meanwhile, melt the butter in a small pan over medium heat. Gradually add the flour, stirring constantly until it has been absorbed. Still stirring, slowly add the milk, until blended. Bring the sauce to a boil, reduce the heat, and simmer, stirring, until it thickens. Add the cheese, mustard, and cayenne pepper (if using), stirring until well blended. Pour the sauce over the eggs and leeks.

Put the dish under the broiler for 2–3 minutes. Serve when bubbling.

mushroom & cauliflower
cheese crumble

		ingredients	
	easy	1 medium cauliflower	1²⁄₃ cups dry bread crumbs
		¼ cup butter, plus 2 tbsp	2 tbsp grated Parmesan cheese
	serves 4	for topping	1 tsp dried oregano
		1²⁄₃ cups sliced white mushrooms	1 tsp dried parsley
		salt and pepper	
	10 minutes		
	20 minutes		

Bring a large pan of salted water to a boil.

Break the cauliflower into small florets and cook in the boiling water for 3 minutes. Remove from the heat, drain well, and transfer to a large, shallow ovenproof dish.

Preheat the oven to 450°F/230°C.

Melt the ¼ cup butter in a small skillet over medium heat. Add the sliced mushrooms, stir to coat, and cook gently for 3 minutes. Remove from the heat and add to the cauliflower. Season with salt and pepper.

Combine the bread crumbs, cheese, and herbs in a small mixing bowl, then sprinkle the crumbs over the vegetables.

Dice the butter for the topping and dot it over the crumbs.

Place the dish in the oven and bake for 15 minutes, or until the crumbs are golden brown and crisp. Serve from the dish.

chile broccoli pasta

very easy	
serves 4	
10 minutes	
20 minutes	

ingredients

2 cups dry penne or macaroni
1 medium head broccoli
¼ cup extra virgin olive oil
2 large garlic cloves, chopped
2 fresh red chiles, seeded
  and diced

8 cherry tomatoes (optional)

small handful of fresh basil or parsley,
  to garnish

Cook the penne or other pasta in a large pan of salted boiling water for about 10 minutes, until al dente. Remove from the heat, drain, rinse with cold water, and drain again. Set aside.

Cut the broccoli into florets and cook in salted boiling water for 5 minutes. Drain, rinse with cold water, and drain again.

Heat the olive oil in the pan that the pasta was cooked in. Add the garlic, chiles, and tomatoes, if using. Cook over high heat for 1 minute.

Return the broccoli to the pan with the oil and mix well. Cook for 2 minutes to heat through. Add the pasta and mix well again. Cook for 1 minute more.

Remove the pasta from the heat, turn into a large serving bowl, and serve garnished with basil or parsley.

leek & spinach pie

		ingredients	
easy	8 oz/225 g puff pastry	2 eggs
	2 tbsp sweet butter	1¼ cups heavy cream
serves 6–8	2 leeks, sliced finely	pinch of dried thyme
	8 oz/225 g spinach, chopped	salt and pepper
20 minutes		
45 minutes + 10 minutes resting time		

Roll the pastry into a rectangle about 10 x 12 inches/25 x 30 cm. Let rest for 5 minutes, then press into a 8 x 10 inch/20 x 25 cm quiche pan. Do not trim the overhang. Cover the pastry with aluminum foil and chill in the refrigerator.

Preheat the oven to 350°F/180°C.

Melt the butter in a large skillet over medium heat. Add the leeks, stir, and cook gently for 5 minutes, or until soft. Add the spinach and cook for 3 minutes, or until soft. Let cool.

Beat the eggs in a bowl. Stir in the cream and season with thyme, salt, and pepper. Remove the pie shell and uncover. Spread the cooked vegetables over the bottom. Pour in the egg mixture.

Place on a cookie sheet and bake for 30 minutes, or until set. Remove the flan from the oven and let it rest for 10 minutes before serving. Serve directly from the quiche pan.

middle eastern
baked eggplant

easy	
serves 4	
15 minutes	
1¼–2¼ hours	

ingredients

1¼ cups olive oil	2 tbsp chopped fresh parsley
1 lb/450 g onions, sliced thinly	2 tbsp chopped fresh basil
6 garlic cloves, sliced thinly	2 eggplants
14 oz/400 g canned	juice of 1 lemon
chopped tomatoes	water to cover
pinch of sugar	
1 tsp salt	lemon wedges, to garnish

Heat 4 tablespoons of the oil over high heat in a large skillet. Stir in the onions and garlic, reduce the heat, and cook until soft but not brown. Add the tomatoes, raise the heat until the mixture boils, then reduce the heat, and simmer for 5 minutes. Add the sugar, salt, and herbs. Preheat the oven to 325°F/160°C.

Cut the eggplants in half lengthwise. Place in a large, ovenproof dish, cut side up. Spoon the onion and tomato mixture on top. Sprinkle with lemon juice, and pour over the remaining olive oil.

Add enough water just to cover the topping, then cover the dish, put in the oven, and bake gently for 1–2 hours, or until soft. Check frequently during the cooking time, pressing down or adding more water if necessary.

Remove from the oven, but leave in the dish to cool. To serve, transfer to a serving dish and garnish with lemon wedges.

stuffed eggplant slices

easy	
serves 4	
10 minutes	
20 minutes + 15 minutes for the sauce	

ingredients

1 medium eggplant
4 tbsp extra virgin olive oil
1 cup grated mozzarella cheese
1 tbsp fresh chopped basil

1 quantity simple tomato sauce (see page 76)

extra basil leaves, to garnish

Preheat the oven to 400°F/200°C.

Slice the eggplant lengthwise into 8 slices. Brush the slices with oil and place on a cookie sheet. Bake for 10 minutes, without letting them get too floppy. Remove from the oven.

Sprinkle the grated cheese and basil over the eggplant slices. Roll up each slice and place the slices in a single layer in a shallow ovenproof dish.

Pour the tomato sauce over them and cook in the oven for 10 minutes or until the sauce bubbles and the cheese melts.

Remove the stuffed eggplant slices from the oven and transfer carefully to serving plates. Spoon the sauce around and on top of each one. Garnish with basil leaves and serve while still hot.

cheese baked zucchini

		ingredients	
very easy	4 medium zucchini	2 large tomatoes, seeded and diced
	2 tbsp extra virgin olive oil	2 tsp chopped fresh oregano or basil
	4 oz/115 g mozzarella cheese,	
serves 4	sliced thinly	a few fresh basil leaves, to garnish
5 minutes		
15 minutes		

Preheat the oven to 400°F/200°C.

Slice the zucchini lengthwise into 4 strips each. Brush with oil and place on a cookie sheet.

Bake the zucchini in the oven for 10 minutes without letting them get too floppy.

Remove the zucchini from the oven. Arrange the slices of cheese on top and sprinkle with diced tomato and basil or oregano. Return to the oven for 5 minutes, or until the cheese melts.

Remove the zucchini from the oven and transfer carefully to serving plates. Serve garnished with fresh basil leaves.

stuffed baked potatoes

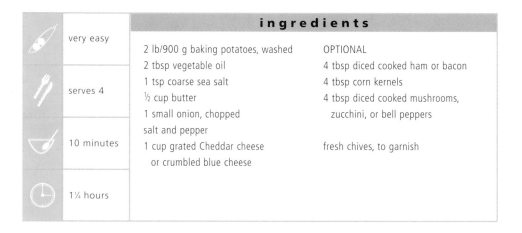

		ingredients	
very easy	2 lb/900 g baking potatoes, washed	OPTIONAL	
	2 tbsp vegetable oil	4 tbsp diced cooked ham or bacon	
serves 4	1 tsp coarse sea salt	4 tbsp corn kernels	
	½ cup butter	4 tbsp diced cooked mushrooms,	
	1 small onion, chopped	zucchini, or bell peppers	
10 minutes	salt and pepper		
	1 cup grated Cheddar cheese	fresh chives, to garnish	
	or crumbled blue cheese		
1¼ hours			

Preheat the oven to 375°F/190°C.

Prick the potatoes with a fork, brush with oil, sprinkle with salt, and bake on a cookie sheet for about 1 hour, or until the skins are crispy and the inside is soft when pierced with a fork.

Melt 1 tablespoon of butter in a small skillet. Cook the onion gently until soft and golden. Set to one side.

Remove the potatoes from the oven and cut in half lengthwise. Scoop the insides into a large mixing bowl and keep the shells. Turn the oven temperature up to 400°F/200°C.

Coarsely mash the potato and mix in the onion and remaining butter. Add salt and pepper and any of the optional ingredients. Spoon the mixture back into the empty shells. Top with cheese.

Return the potatoes to the oven for 10 minutes, or until the cheese melts and begins to brown. Garnish with chives to serve.

bell peppers stuffed
with rice & corn

		ingredients	
easy		4 red or green bell peppers	2 tbsp chopped fresh cilantro
		1⅓ cups cooked rice	¼ tsp salt
serves 4		¾ cup corn kernels	2 tbsp olive oil
		½ tsp cayenne pepper, chili powder,	7 oz/200 g canned chopped tomatoes
10 minutes		or chili pepper flakes	
60 minutes			

Preheat the oven to 375°F/190°C.

Cut a slice off the top of each bell pepper and discard. Carefully remove all the seeds from inside the bell peppers. Closely pack the bell peppers, upright, in a casserole.

Combine the rice, corn, spices, cilantro, and salt in a large mixing bowl, reserving a little corn and cilantro to use as garnish. Carefully spoon the mixture into the bell peppers.

Drizzle olive oil over the top of each bell pepper. Pour the tomatoes over them.

Place the casserole in the oven and bake the bell peppers for 1 hour, or until soft. Remove from the oven and either let cool in the casserole or carefully lift out and arrange on serving plates. Spoon the tomatoes and juices from the dish over the bell peppers. Serve garnished with the reserved corn and cilantro.

caramelized onion tart

	ingredients	
easy	7 tbsp sweet butter	scant 1 cup grated Swiss cheese
	lb 5 oz/600 g onions, thinly sliced	8 inch/20 cm baked pie shell
serves 4–6	2 eggs	generous 1 cup grated
	scant ½ cup heavy cream	Parmesan cheese
	salt and pepper	
10 minutes		
45–55 minutes + 10 minutes resting time		

Melt the butter over medium heat in a heavy skillet. Stir in the onions and cook until they are well browned and caramelized. (This will take up to 30 minutes, depending on the depth of the skillet.) Stir frequently to avoid burning. Remove the onions from the skillet and set aside.

Preheat the oven to 375°F/190°C.

Beat the eggs in a large mixing bowl, stir in the cream, and season with salt and pepper. Add the Swiss cheese and mix well. Mix in the cooked onions.

Pour the egg and onion mixture into the baked pie shell, sprinkle with Parmesan, and place on a cookie sheet. Bake for 15–20 minutes, or until the filling has set and begun to brown.

Remove from the oven and let rest for at least 10 minutes. The tart can be served hot or let cool to room temperature.

bubble & squeak

very easy	
serves 4	
20 minutes	
60 minutes	

ingredients

1 lb/450 g mealy potatoes,
  peeled and diced
2 tbsp milk
¼ cup butter
salt and pepper

2½ cups shredded green cabbage
1½ cups thinly sliced carrots
1 medium onion, chopped
½ cup grated Cheddar cheese

Cook the potatoes in salted water for 10 minutes, or until soft. Drain well and turn into a large mixing bowl. Mash until smooth. Beat with the milk, half the butter, and salt and pepper to taste.

Cook the cabbage and carrots separately in salted boiling water for 5 minutes. Drain well. Combine the cabbage with the potatoes.

Melt the remaining butter in a small skillet and cook the onion over medium heat until soft but not brown.

Preheat the oven to 375°F/190°C.

Spread a layer of mashed potatoes in the bottom of a greased shallow ovenproof dish. Layer onions on top, then carrots. Repeat to use up all the ingredients, finishing with a layer of potato.

Sprinkle the grated cheese on top, place the dish in the oven, and bake for 45 minutes, or until the top is golden and crusty. Remove from the oven and serve immediately.

side
dishes

A side dish of vegetables can lift an ordinary meal into the realms of haute cuisine. You can create a balance through your choice: contrast a simple main course with a complex or exotic side dish or temper a more complicated main course with a straightforward plate of fresh, steamed, seasonal vegetables. Aim for an overall balance of textures, flavors, and even colors. Use these surprisingly easy recipes—and your flair and imagination—to transform any meal you decide to serve.

crispy roast asparagus

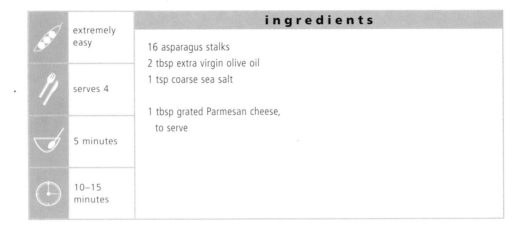

		ingredients
	extremely easy	16 asparagus stalks
	serves 4	2 tbsp extra virgin olive oil
		1 tsp coarse sea salt
	5 minutes	1 tbsp grated Parmesan cheese, to serve
	10–15 minutes	

Preheat the oven to 400°F/200°C.

Choose asparagus stalks of similar widths. Trim the base of the stalks so that all the stems are approximately the same length.

Arrange the asparagus in a single layer on a cookie sheet. Drizzle with olive oil and sprinkle with salt.

Place the cookie sheet in the oven and bake for 10–15 minutes, turning once. Remove from the oven, transfer to an attractive dish, and serve immediately, sprinkled with the grated Parmesan.

barley & mushroom pilaf

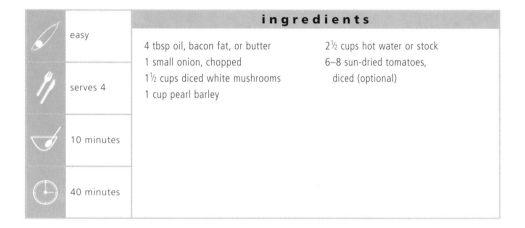

		ingredients	
easy	4 tbsp oil, bacon fat, or butter	2½ cups hot water or stock	
	1 small onion, chopped	6–8 sun-dried tomatoes,	
serves 4	1½ cups diced white mushrooms	diced (optional)	
	1 cup pearl barley		
10 minutes			
40 minutes			

Heat the oil or bacon fat or melt the butter in a deep pan over low heat.

Stir in the onion and cook gently until soft and starting to turn golden. Do not let brown.

Add the mushrooms and stir well. Cook gently for 5 minutes.

Add the barley and mix well to coat. Continue cooking over medium heat for 5 minutes to color slightly.

Pour in the hot liquid, stir, and bring to a boil. Reduce the heat, cover the pan, and cook gently until all the liquid has been absorbed (about 25 minutes).

If you are using sun-dried tomatoes, stir most of them into the pilaf just before serving and sprinkle a few extra pieces over the top as a garnish.

sweet & sour
vegetable combo

easy	
serves 4	
10 minutes	
25–35 minutes	

ingredients

1 medium carrot, thickly sliced
1 cup pumpkin or butternut squash, thickly sliced
1 medium zucchini, thickly sliced
1 medium leek, thickly sliced
2 tsp cornstarch
1 tsp sugar

2 tsp wine vinegar
3 tsp sweet sherry
1¼ cups water
3 tsp tomato paste
6 pieces preserved ginger, diced
1 tbsp ginger syrup

Bring a large pan of salted water to a boil. Reduce the heat slightly so that the water is just simmering.

Place the carrots and pumpkin in a blanching basket or steamer. Cook in or over the boiling water for 5–10 minutes, or until just softening. Transfer to a shallow ovenproof dish.

Blanch or steam the zucchini for 3–5 minutes, or until just beginning to soften. Add to the carrots and pumpkin.

Blanch or steam the leek for 2 minutes in the same way. Add to the other vegetables. Mix thoroughly.

Preheat the oven to 325°F/160°C.

Mix the cornstarch and sugar in a small bowl. Add the vinegar and sherry, stirring to make a smooth paste. Gradually stir in the water and tomato paste, then the ginger and syrup. Stir the mixture into the vegetables. Bake for 15 minutes. Serve immediately.

mustard broccoli polonaise

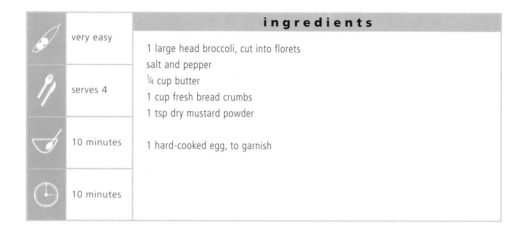

		ingredients
very easy		1 large head broccoli, cut into florets
		salt and pepper
serves 4		¼ cup butter
		1 cup fresh bread crumbs
		1 tsp dry mustard powder
10 minutes		1 hard-cooked egg, to garnish
10 minutes		

Bring a large pan of salted water to a boil. Add the broccoli to the pan, cook for 5 minutes, or until tender, then drain, rinse in cold water, and drain once more. Transfer to a large serving dish. Season to taste with salt and pepper.

While the broccoli is cooking, melt the butter in a skillet and toss in the bread crumbs until well coated. Cook for 1 minute, or until the crumbs start to get brown and crisp, then stir in the mustard powder.

Remove the bread crumbs from the heat and sprinkle them over the broccoli.

Peel and finely grate the hard-cooked egg. Sprinkle it over the bread crumbs to garnish. Serve while still hot.

baby fava beans
with rice

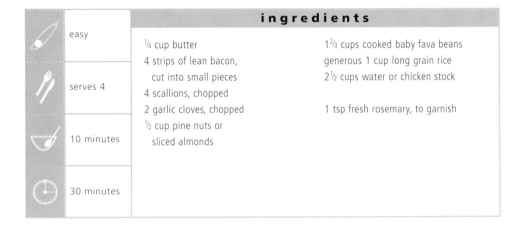

		ingredients	
easy		¼ cup butter	1⅔ cups cooked baby fava beans
		4 strips of lean bacon,	generous 1 cup long grain rice
serves 4		cut into small pieces	2½ cups water or chicken stock
		4 scallions, chopped	
		2 garlic cloves, chopped	1 tsp fresh rosemary, to garnish
10 minutes		½ cup pine nuts or	
		sliced almonds	
30 minutes			

Melt the butter over medium heat in a deep pan and cook the bacon gently until crisp. Remove with a slotted spoon and set aside. Soften the scallions and garlic in the fat remaining in the pan. Drain and add them to the bacon.

Toss the pine nuts and fava beans in the pan for 1–2 minutes over medium heat. Add the rice and stir to coat.

Return the other cooked ingredients to the pan. Mix well.

Add the water (or stock, if using) to the pan, turn up the heat, and bring to a boil. Reduce the heat to low, cover the pan, and cook for 20 minutes. Check halfway through the cooking time and add more water if the mixture is drying out too much.

When the rice is soft, stir the mixture well, and transfer to a serving dish. Serve garnished with rosemary.

classic roast vegetables

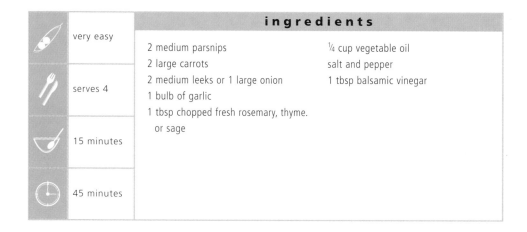

		ingredients	
very easy		2 medium parsnips	¼ cup vegetable oil
		2 large carrots	salt and pepper
serves 4		2 medium leeks or 1 large onion	1 tbsp balsamic vinegar
		1 bulb of garlic	
15 minutes		1 tbsp chopped fresh rosemary, thyme.	
		or sage	
45 minutes			

Preheat the oven to 450°F/230°C.

Peel the parsnips and cut off the narrow top end. Cut this in half lengthwise. Slice the bases lengthwise, then cut each piece into smaller strips.

Cut the carrots and leeks or onion into strips of a similar size.

Separate the cloves of garlic, but do not peel.

Place all the vegetables in a heavy roasting pan. Sprinkle with the chopped herbs and oil and mix together.

Place the pan in the oven and roast the vegetables, stirring occasionally, for 45 minutes, or until soft and brown.

Transfer the vegetables to a large serving dish, season to taste with salt and pepper, sprinkle with balsamic vinegar, and serve.

curried cauliflower
& tomatoes

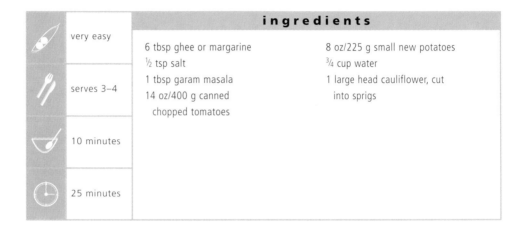

		ingredients	
	very easy	6 tbsp ghee or margarine	8 oz/225 g small new potatoes
		½ tsp salt	¾ cup water
	serves 3–4	1 tbsp garam masala	1 large head cauliflower, cut
		14 oz/400 g canned	into sprigs
	10 minutes	chopped tomatoes	
	25 minutes		

Melt the ghee or margarine over medium heat in a large pan. Stir in the salt, garam masala, and the tomatoes with their juices.

Bring the mixture to a boil, reduce the heat, and simmer gently for 5 minutes.

Add the whole potatoes and the water and stir well. Simmer for 5 more minutes.

Add the cauliflower to the pan and stir well. Cook for 15 minutes longer, checking regularly to make sure that the vegetables don't get too soft. Transfer to a serving dish, or serve the vegetables straight from the pan.

crispy spinach
& bacon

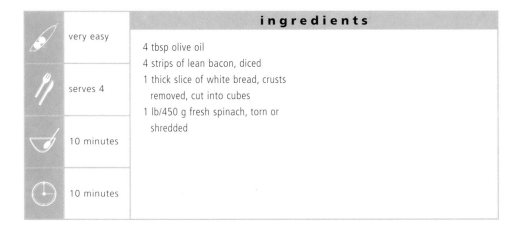

		ingredients
very easy		4 tbsp olive oil
		4 strips of lean bacon, diced
serves 4		1 thick slice of white bread, crusts
		removed, cut into cubes
		1 lb/450 g fresh spinach, torn or
10 minutes		shredded
10 minutes		

Heat 2 tablespoons of the olive oil over high heat in a large skillet. Add the diced bacon to the skillet and cook for 3–4 minutes, or until crisp. Remove with a slotted spoon, draining carefully, and set aside.

Toss the cubes of bread in the fat remaining in the skillet over high heat for about 4 minutes, or until crisp and golden. Remove the croûtons with a slotted spoon, draining carefully, and set them aside.

Add the remaining oil to the skillet and heat. Toss the spinach in the oil over high heat for about 3 minutes, or until it has just wilted. Turn into a serving bowl and sprinkle with the bacon and croûtons. Serve immediately.

lemon & garlic spinach

		ingredients
very easy		4 tbsp olive oil
serves 4		2 garlic cloves, thinly sliced
		1 lb/450 g fresh spinach, torn or
		shredded
5 minutes		juice of ½ lemon
		salt and pepper
10 minutes		

Heat the olive oil in a large skillet over high heat. Add the garlic and spinach and cook, stirring constantly, until the spinach is soft. Take care not to let the spinach burn.

Remove from the heat, turn into a serving bowl, and sprinkle with lemon juice. Season with salt and pepper. Mix well and serve either hot or at room temperature.

carrots in marsala
cream sauce

		ingredients	
very easy	1 lb/450 g carrots	2 tbsp raisins
	½ cup sweet butter	¼ cup Marsala
serves 4	¼ cup brown sugar	¼ cup light cream
10 minutes		
15 minutes		

Peel the carrots and cut into 2 inch/5 cm pieces. Blanch for 3 minutes in salted boiling water. Remove from the heat, drain, and set aside.

Melt the butter over medium heat in a heavy skillet. Add the sugar and stir until it has dissolved.

Add the raisins to the butter and sugar mixture. Stir well and simmer gently for 2 minutes, or until the raisins are plump.

Pour the Marsala into the butter mixture, increase the heat until it boils, then lower to simmering point. Add the carrots, stir well, and cook for 5 minutes to heat through and soften.

Remove the skillet from the heat, stir in the cream, and transfer the carrots to a serving dish.

trio of puréed vegetables

easy	
serves 4	
20 minutes	
25–35 minutes	

ingredients

1 lb/450 g mealy potatoes, peeled and cut into chunks
6 tbsp butter
¼ cup warm milk
1 tsp wholegrain mustard
salt and pepper

1 lb/450 g rutabaga or parsnips, peeled and cut into chunks
1 tbsp chopped fresh parsley
1 lb/450 g carrots, peeled and cut into chunks
1 tbsp chopped fresh cilantro

Put the potato pieces in a large pan of cold water, bring to a boil, then reduce the heat, and simmer for 10–15 minutes, until the potatoes are soft. Drain well and mash with 2 tablespoons of butter. Stir in the milk and mustard, then season to taste with salt and pepper. Turn into a serving dish and keep warm.

Meanwhile, put the rutabaga or parsnips in a large pan of cold water, bring to a boil, and simmer for 15–20 minutes, until soft. Drain and mash with 2 tablespoons of butter. Season with salt and pepper. Stir in the parsley. Turn into a serving dish and keep warm.

At the same time, cook the carrot chunks in the same way, simmering for 10–15 minutes, until soft. Drain well and mash with the remaining 2 tablespoons of butter. Season to taste. Stir in the cilantro. Turn into a serving dish and keep warm.

Serve the three vegetables with your favorite roast.

herbed potato stew

very easy	
serves 4	
10 minutes	
45 minutes	

ingredients

2 tbsp olive oil
1 medium onion, sliced thinly
2 garlic cloves, sliced thinly
1 green bell pepper, seeded and sliced
14 oz/400 g canned
  chopped tomatoes

4 mealy potatoes, peeled and cubed
1½ cups water
salt and pepper
2 tsp chopped fresh thyme
1 bay leaf

Heat the olive oil over medium heat in a large heavy pan. Stir in the onion, garlic, and green bell pepper. Cook for 10 minutes, just to soften.

Add the tomatoes to the pan and bring to a boil. Reduce the heat so that the mixture is just simmering and stir until most of the liquid has been absorbed (about 5 minutes).

Add the potatoes, water, salt, pepper, thyme, and bay leaf. Cover the pan, reduce the heat, and cook gently for 30 minutes, or until the potatoes are beginning to fall apart. Stir occasionally.

Remove the pan from the heat, discard the bay leaf, and spoon the stew into a serving dish.

potato pancakes

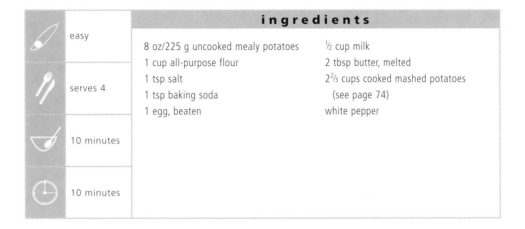

		ingredients	
easy	8 oz/225 g uncooked mealy potatoes	½ cup milk	
	1 cup all-purpose flour	2 tbsp butter, melted	
serves 4	1 tsp salt	2⅔ cups cooked mashed potatoes	
	1 tsp baking soda	(see page 74)	
10 minutes	1 egg, beaten	white pepper	
10 minutes			

Grate the raw potatoes into a large bowl. Turn into a strainer and drain out all the water and starch, pressing down hard.

Sift the flour with salt and baking soda.

Combine the egg, milk, and melted butter in a small bowl.

Return the grated potatoes to the large bowl, add the mashed potatoes, flour, and egg and milk mixture. Mix thoroughly to make a thick batter. Season with pepper.

Heat a large skillet or flat griddle. Drop spoonfuls of batter into the skillet and flatten slightly. Cook for about 5 minutes, until the bottom is golden, then turn and cook until the second side is golden.

Serve the pancakes hot, to accompany broiled or boiled bacon, ham, or corned beef.

potato biscuits

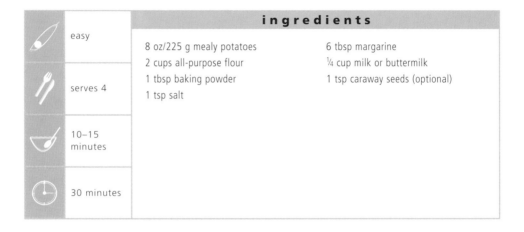

		ingredients	
easy		8 oz/225 g mealy potatoes	6 tbsp margarine
		2 cups all-purpose flour	¼ cup milk or buttermilk
serves 4		1 tbsp baking powder	1 tsp caraway seeds (optional)
		1 tsp salt	
10–15 minutes			
30 minutes			

Peel and dice the potatoes and boil them for about 10 minutes in a large pan of salted water. When they are soft, drain, turn into a large mixing bowl, and mash until smooth. Let cool slightly.

Preheat the oven to 450°F/230°C.

Sift the flour, baking powder, and salt into a mixing bowl. Rub in the margarine until the mixture resembles coarse bread crumbs. Add the mashed potatoes and mix with just enough milk to bind into a dough.

Turn the dough onto a floured counter and roll out until it is approximately ½ inch/1 cm thick. Cut into rounds or squares.

Place the biscuits on a greased cookie sheet. If you are using caraway seeds, sprinkle them on top.

Transfer the cookie sheet to the oven. Bake for 20 minutes, or until well risen. Remove from the oven and serve immediately.

simple tomato sauce

		ingredients	

very easy		14 oz/400 g canned
		  chopped tomatoes
		½ tsp dried oregano
		½ tsp dried basil
		½ tsp salt
		½–1 tsp dried chili flakes or
		  1 small fresh chile, seeded
		  and chopped finely
			OPTIONAL
			½ tsp garlic powder
			pinch of fennel seeds
			pinch of sugar

serves 4			
5 minutes			
15 minutes			

Combine the tomatoes, herbs, salt, and chili flakes or fresh chile in a small pan.

Add the garlic powder, fennel seeds, and sugar, if using. Bring to a boil, reduce the heat, and simmer gently for 15 minutes. Taste for seasoning and adjust if necessary.

The sauce can be made in advance and reheated when you are ready to use it. Serve with pasta, as a topping for pizza, or to cook meatballs and Italian sausages.

battered vegetable fritters

easy	
serves 4	
10 minutes	
20 minutes	

ingredients

2 medium zucchini
1 small eggplant
8 white mushrooms (optional)
8 baby corn, blanched (optional)
1 sweet onion, sliced and
    separated into rings (optional)
vegetable oil for deep-frying

BATTER
1 cup all-purpose flour
1 egg, beaten
½ cup water
pinch of salt
pinch of sugar
pinch of dried oregano

fresh basil, to garnish

Trim the zucchini. Slice them lengthwise, then cut each slice into long strips.

Trim the eggplant. Slice thinly lengthwise, then cut into strips.

Put enough oil into a deep-fryer or wok to deep-fry and place over high heat.

Sift the flour and mix with the beaten egg and water to make a thick batter. Stir in the salt, sugar, and oregano.

Dip pieces of vegetable in batter, lift out, and drain off any excess, then lower into the hot oil. Fry for 2–3 minutes, or until crisp and golden. Remove the vegetables from the oil with a slotted spoon and drain on paper towels. Keep warm while you cook the remaining slices and any optional vegetables. Serve while very hot, garnished with sprigs of fresh basil.

crispy vegetable pancakes

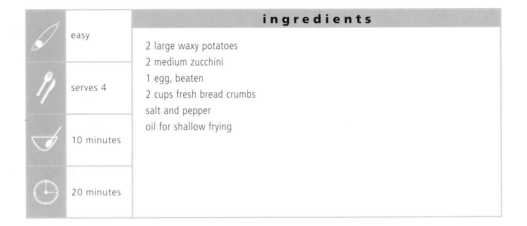

		ingredients
easy		2 large waxy potatoes
		2 medium zucchini
serves 4		1 egg, beaten
		2 cups fresh bread crumbs
		salt and pepper
10 minutes		oil for shallow frying
20 minutes		

Peel and grate the potatoes. Turn into a strainer and drain out all the water and starch, pressing down hard.

Trim the zucchini and grate into a large bowl.

Combine the grated potatoes with the zucchini. Mix the egg and bread crumbs into the vegetables and season with salt and pepper to taste.

Heat the oil in a large skillet. Drop spoonfuls of the vegetable mixture into the hot oil and press down gently to make pancakes.

Fry the pancakes over high heat for 5–10 minutes (depending on their thickness), until the bottom is golden brown and crispy. Turn and cook until the second side is brown and crispy. Lift out gently, drain on paper towels, place on a serving dish, and keep warm until all the pancakes are cooked. Serve immediately.

braised fennel fiorentina

		ingredients
	very easy	2 bulbs of fresh fennel
		2 tbsp olive oil
	serves 4	juice of 1 lemon
		1 tsp sugar
	5 minutes	salt and pepper
	25 minutes	

Cut the fennel in half lengthwise and then into wedges.

Heat the oil over medium heat in a heavy pan large enough to take all the fennel wedges in a single layer. Place the fennel pieces in the pan and brown in the oil, stirring occasionally. Sprinkle with lemon juice, sugar, salt, and pepper. Stir once.

Bring the liquid in the pan to a boil, cover, reduce the heat to low, and simmer gently for 20 minutes. Check and stir occasionally, adding a very small amount of water if necessary to prevent the fennel from sticking. There should be just enough juice left at the end of the cooking time to glaze the fennel lightly.

Remove the pan from the heat and transfer the cooked fennel to a serving dish. Spoon the juice from the pan over it and let cool slightly.

Serve at room temperature.

cheese baked fennel

very easy	
serves 4	
10 minutes	
60 minutes	

ingredients

2 tbsp sweet butter
2 bulbs of fresh fennel
4 tbsp grated Swiss cheese
1¼ cups light cream
1 tbsp wholegrain mustard

pinch ground nutmeg
salt and pepper
2 tbsp fresh bread crumbs
2 tbsp grated Parmesan cheese

Preheat the oven to 350°F/180°C.

Butter a shallow ovenproof dish.

Cut the fennel in half lengthwise and then cut into wedges. Arrange half the wedges in a layer, cut side up, in the dish.

Scatter half the Swiss cheese over the fennel. Place the remaining fennel on top and cover with another layer of cheese.

Mix the cream with the mustard, nutmeg, salt, and pepper. Pour the mixture over the fennel.

Combine the bread crumbs and Parmesan. Sprinkle this over the fennel and pat down gently.

Place the dish in the oven and bake for 1 hour, or until the fennel feels soft when pierced with a fork or skewer. Remove from the oven and serve directly from the dish.

caramelized sweet potatoes

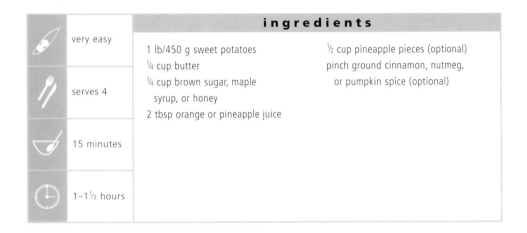

	very easy
	serves 4
	15 minutes
	1–1½ hours

ingredients

1 lb/450 g sweet potatoes
¼ cup butter
¼ cup brown sugar, maple
  syrup, or honey
2 tbsp orange or pineapple juice

½ cup pineapple pieces (optional)
pinch ground cinnamon, nutmeg,
  or pumpkin spice (optional)

Wash the sweet potatoes, but do not peel. Boil them in a large pan of salted water until just tender, for about 30–45 minutes depending on their size. Remove from the heat and drain well. Cool slightly, then peel.

Preheat the oven to 400°F/200°C.

Thickly slice the sweet potatoes and arrange in a single over-lapping layer in a greased ovenproof dish. Cut the butter into small cubes and dot them over the top.

Sprinkle with the sugar, maple syrup or honey and the fruit juice. Add the pineapple and spices, if using.

Bake for 30–40 minutes, basting occasionally, until golden brown.

Serve with baked ham or roast turkey.

brussels sprouts
with chestnuts

		ingredients
	very easy	1 lb/450 g Brussels sprouts ½ cup sweet butter ¼ cup brown sugar ½ cup cooked and shelled chestnuts
	serves 4	
	10 minutes	
	20 minutes	

Bring a large pan of salted water to a boil over high heat.

Trim the Brussels sprouts, removing the coarse stems and any loose outer leaves. Add to the pan of water and boil for 5–10 minutes until just cooked but not too soft. Drain well, rinse in cold water, and drain again. Set aside.

Melt the butter in a heavy skillet. Add the sugar and stir over medium heat until dissolved.

Add the chestnuts to the skillet and cook, stirring occasionally, until they are well coated and starting to brown.

Add the sprouts to the skillet with the chestnuts and mix well. Reduce the heat and cook gently, stirring occasionally, for 3–4 minutes to heat through.

Remove from the heat, transfer to a serving dish, and serve with your favorite roast.

bacon & onion sprouts

		ingredients
	very easy	1 lb/450 g Brussels sprouts
	serves 4	½ cup butter
		4 strips of lean bacon, diced
		1 small onion, chopped coarsely
	10 minutes	
	20 minutes	

Bring a large pan of salted water to a boil over high heat.

Trim the Brussels sprouts, removing the coarse stems and any loose outer leaves. Add to the pan of water and cook for 5–10 minutes, or until just cooked but not too soft. Drain well, rinse in cold water, and drain again. Set aside.

Melt the butter in a heavy skillet. Add the bacon and cook over medium heat until crisp and brown, stirring occasionally. Remove the bacon with a slotted spoon, draining well, and set aside.

Add the chopped onion to the skillet, stir once to coat, and cook over medium heat until soft but not brown.

Add the sprouts to the onion and stir well to coat. Reduce the heat and cook gently for 3–4 minutes to heat through.

Transfer to a serving dish and sprinkle with the cooked bacon.

caraway red cabbage
with apples

		ingredients	
very easy		4 tbsp bacon, chicken, goose, or duck fat	2 large cooking apples, sliced
		2 tbsp sugar	2 tbsp red wine vinegar
serves 4–6		1 small onion, chopped finely	1 tsp caraway seeds
		5 cups coarsely shredded red cabbage	
10 minutes			
25–30 minutes			

Melt the fat over high heat in a large heavy skillet.

Sprinkle in the sugar and stir until it browns. Add the onion and continue to cook, stirring constantly, until golden.

Add the cabbage and apples. Mix well to coat with fat and sugar. Sprinkle in the vinegar and caraway seeds.

Cover the skillet and cook over low heat for about 20 minutes, or until the cabbage is as tender as you want it. Stir occasionally and add 2–3 tablespoons of water during the cooking time, if necessary, to prevent the cabbage from sticking.

Remove from the skillet and transfer to a serving dish. Serve as an accompaniment to pork, venison, or sausages.

rösti

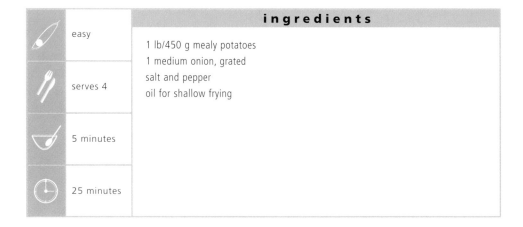

		ingredients
easy		1 lb/450 g mealy potatoes
		1 medium onion, grated
serves 4		salt and pepper
		oil for shallow frying
5 minutes		
25 minutes		

Wash the potatoes, but do not peel them. Place in a large pan, cover with water, and bring to a boil, covered, over high heat. Reduce the heat and simmer for about 10 minutes, until the potatoes are just beginning to soften. Be careful not to overcook.

Drain the potatoes. Let cool, then peel, and grate coarsely. Mix the grated onion with the potatoes. Season the mixture with salt and pepper.

Heat the oil in a heavy skillet and spoon in the potato mixture. The rösti can be as thick or as thin as you like, and can be made into 1 large cake or several individual ones.

Cook over high heat for about 5 minutes, until the bottom is golden, then turn, and cook until the second side is brown and crispy. Remove from the heat, drain, and serve.

index